Andrew J. Pritt

C000214173

Return to Ryde by Steam

Volume 2

Andrew Britton

Commemorating the 40th anniversary of the final full year of railway operation of the Ryde-Newport-Cowes and Ryde-Sandown-Shanklin-Ventnor lines.

"HOW CAN YOU FOLLOW THE QUALITY and the standards you have set in 'Ryde by Steam Volume One'?" was the question put to me in the BBC studio in Southampton. Well here is the answer: 'Return to Ryde by Steam Volume Two'. Not only will the pictures contained in this colour series be preserved in the public domain, but the royalties from the photographer's reproduction fees will be donated towards the overhaul of 24 Calbourne at the Isle of Wight Steam Railway.

The photographers who have contributed towards this book are the real heroes and their work is to be praised. We owe them so much for having the foresight and dedication to photograph in colour the scenes reproduced in this book. They include: R. J. Blenkinsop, Peter Paye, Tim R. Genower, Dr. J. Mackett, R. E. 'Bob' Burroughs, A. E. Bennett, Iain E. Whitlam, Roy Hobbs, David Janes, David Peters, Tim Stephens, Graham S. Cocks and Barry J. Eagles. Special thanks must also be extended to Mrs. Chris Westcott daughter of the late H. P. Mason who placed her late father's photographic archives at my disposal for this project. Peter Mason undertook a unique colour study of every railway station on the Island, including those closed prior to 1956. Additionally, Colin Elvers also offered his extensive photographic collection in addition to rallying the residents of Ventnor to assist with research. Ron White, 'Mr Colour Rail', deserves a very special mention for he generously placed the entire Colour Rail Isle of Wight archive at my disposal. Colour Rail can be recommended as the best way to preserve railway colour photographic material in the public domain for future generations. Hopefully, Ron's generous offer will be taken up further in the next book, which focuses on the 1950s/early 60s, the closed pre 1956 branches and explores the Island E1 and O2 tanks in greater depth.

Considerable assistance was obtained from David Unitt, a distinguished national vintage motor vehicle expert, who freely gave up his valuable time to assist with research for this book. Many former Island railway staff from steam days helped enormously with putting names to faces and locations including: Ken West, John Howe, Peter Mills, Terry Hatcher, Tony Tiltman, Sam Wells and Ron Russell. Richard Maycock, Tim Genower John Edgington and Tim Cooper also offered their valuable expertise. The loan of the Charles Woodnutt diaries from the Isle of Wight Steam Railway Museum and the acquisition of the working timetables/rostering duties/signal box train registers and notes of the late drivers Harry 'Toby' Watson and Jim Hunnybun were the icing on the cake. Sincere thanks too to Christine Mackett for her generous hospitality whilst on the Island (still the best coffee on the Island).

A huge thank you must be extended to Mike Lambert, Dan Wood, Shelley Harris, Sue Loudoun, Graham Attrill and the team at Crossprint Design & Print at Newport on the Isle of Wight. It is their expertise that has ensured the quality of the reproduction and design of both this book and 'Ryde by Steam Volume One'. They have spent countless hours cleaning and preparing slides in order to achieve superior digital reproduction of the slides.

I offer my sincere thanks to R. J. 'Dick' Blenkinsop who has continued to be my mentor and inspiration. He not only encourages and offers constructive professional advice through his years in railway photography, but is also a true Island railway enthusiast.

My thanks too to Mike, Ruth and James Pringle for all their hours of hard work with the cover design and website, not forgetting my wife Annette, sons Jonathan, Mark & Matthew and my mother, Joan, for their continued patience and support.

Copyright 2005 Medina Books   ISBN   0-9548507-1-8   All rights reserved. No part of this book may be reproduced or transmitted in any form or by any means, electronic or mechanical, including photocopying, recording or any information storage or retrieval system without the prior permission from the Publisher.

Printed by Crossprint Design & Print, Newport Business Park, 21 Barry Way, Newport, Isle of Wight, PO30 5GY
Published by Medina Books, 1 Landor Road, Warwick, CV34 5DU

Front cover: 'Gateway to the Isle of Wight'. This is the scene which would have welcomed generations of passengers at Ryde Pier Head station. Standing in Platform 2, in the final summer of steam working in July 1966, is 35 Freshwater, complete with her final temporary painted nameplates, waiting impatiently for the guard's green flag and whistle with a train to Shanklin. We gaze back in time down Ryde Pier as an approaching six coach train passes by the Pier Head signal box. In the foreground on the right are the distinctive upper quadrant signals, whilst in the centre there is the unique starting bell. Partially obscured behind the locomotive is the water tank. This everyday scene has now gone for ever. *R.J. Blenkinsop*

The deck of the Paddle Steamer Sandown is laden with tourists as she departs from Ryde Pier Head for Portsmouth Harbour whilst the next generation of Island ferry, the M.V. Brading, approaches on Saturday 25th July 1964. This was a familiar sight that somehow set the scene for visitors to the Isle of Wight. *Tim Stephens*

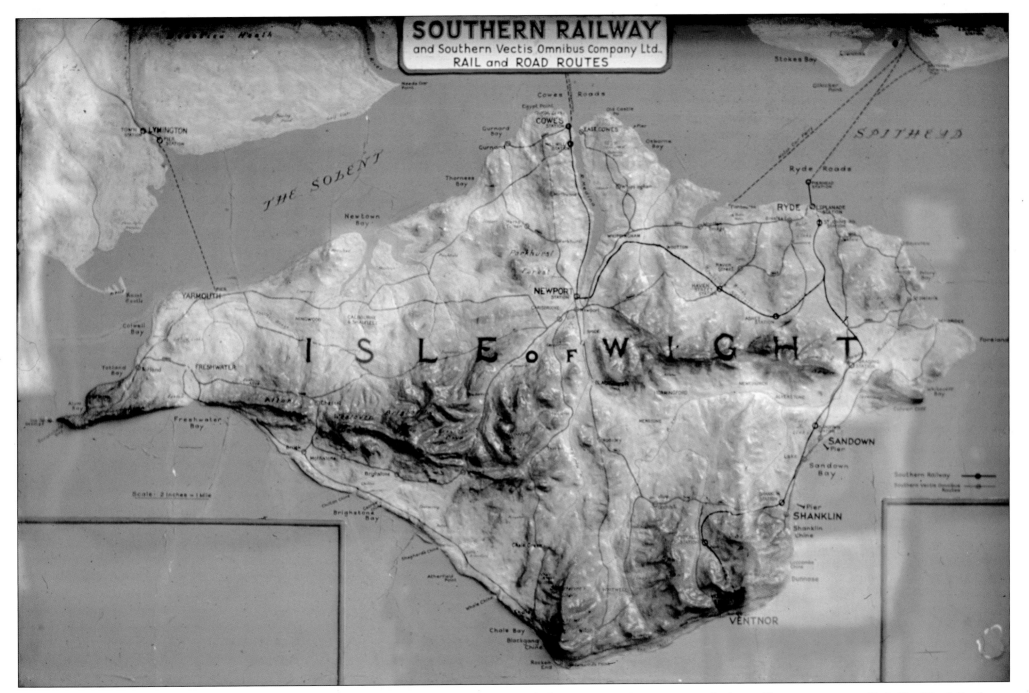

At many Island stations the passengers were provided with a map of the Isle of Wight complete with the road and railway routes marked out. There were maps at Ryde Pier Head, Sandown, Shanklin, Ventnor, Newport and Cowes. This particular map was at Cowes Station and was taken on 13th July 1963. *H.P. Mason*

3

The first view of Ryde Pier Head station seen by the tourist travelling to the Island on the 25th May 1963 was the impressive entrance with the proud canopy and station sign. Having left the boat, train passengers then walked across the station concourse to queue for the next departure. The stations on our routes are clearly listed Platform 3 for the Ventnor and Platform 4 for the Cowes lines. *H. P. Mason*

A footplate welcome by Driver 'Ginger' Minter and Fireman Ray Hobden on board 14 Fishbourne on Friday 5th August 1966, heading away from the Pier Head to return to Ryde by steam! *G. S. Cocks*

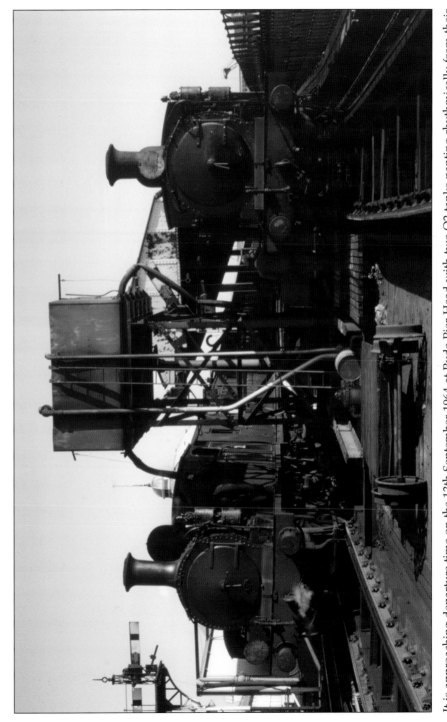

It is approaching departure time on the 13th September 1964 at Ryde Pier Head with two O2 tanks panting rhythmically from their Westinghouse air brake pumps. On the right, at Platform 1, 20 Shanklin prepares to depart with a good head of steam for Ventnor, while on the left 28 Ashey makes ready to leave for Newport and Cowes. All stations Ventnor line bound trains carried one white disc or lamp at the foot of the chimney. The headcode for trains omitting certain stops on the Ventnor line was one disc or lamp below the chimney and one at the centre of the buffer beam, whilst Cowes line locomotives had a disc or lamp over each buffer. Fireman Ray Lewns is pictured topping up the tanks on 28 Ashey. During the summer, a popular pastime for footplate crews in between duties at Ryde Pier Head was to go for a refreshing swim under the pier. Station staff have also been photographed fishing, as captured in 'Once Upon A Line Volume Two'. *Roy Hobbs*

 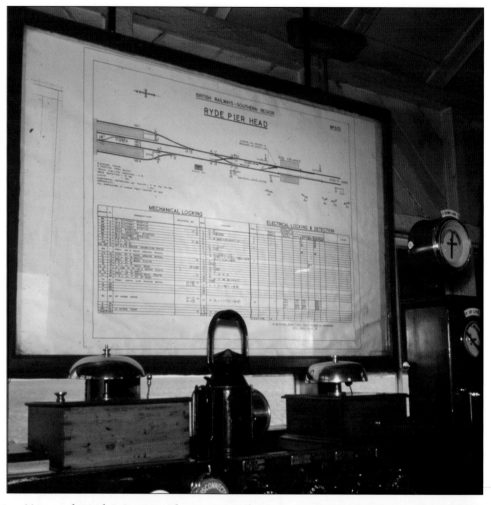

Signalmen John Wells and Eric Fry have been hard at work polishing the levers in Ryde Pier Head signal box on the 24th July 1962. The interior of this box afforded superb views of the Spithead and it was possible to enjoy the sight of passing Atlantic bound liners and Naval Reviews in addition to steam trains. Between the Wars it was also a superb vantage point from which to observe the Schneider Trophy air races, according to the former Southern Railway Pier Head Signalman, Owen Attrill. Above the immaculate lever frame was the signalling and point diagram which covered the section from Ryde Pier Head to Ryde Esplanade Tunnel. *Dr. J. Mackett*

A view looking up the 32 chain Ryde Pier from Ryde Esplanade station. This was the busiest station on the Isle of Wight. It was a beautiful place to work or watch the trains in the summer, but in the winter the waves would blow up from underneath and could lead to suspension of the service on occasions. At times the Pier Head signalman has been cut off for several hours until low tide and a winter storm had subsided. *R.J. Blenkinsop*

The distinguished railway photographer and author of the superb Island railway books, 'Steam On The Isle of Wight 1956-1966' (with Ken Paye), 'Isle of Wight Railways Remembered' and 'The Ventnor West Branch', has captured to perfection 18 Ningwood pulling into Ryde Esplanade with a train for Ventnor. The platform is on a nine chain radius left hand curve with a falling 1 in 50 gradient at the landward end leading to Ryde Tunnel. *Peter Paye*

28 Ashey prepares to depart with a Ventnor bound train at the south end of Ryde Esplanade. Pictured next to the foot crossing is Jimmy James, the outside carpenter, who was better known for his notorious cartoon sketches of the railway staff, many of which are reproduced in the 'Once Upon A Line' books. *R. E. Burroughs*

An outstanding, extraordinary and breathtaking 'master shot' by Dick Blenkinsop taken from Ryde Esplanade looking up Ryde Pier in August 1965. It captures a four coach Cowes bound train heading down the pier past the Pier Head signal box, complete with a passenger luggage van next to the engine. Heading in the opposite direction on the adjacent lines is a Ryde Pier tram. To complete this remarkable scene we can see a six coach Ventnor train back at the Pier Head station. *R. J. Blenkinsop*

Ventnor bound 24 Calbourne heads towards Ryde St John's Road past the site of Ryde Gas Works on the 15th July 1960. This six coach Ventnor train is made up of a mixture of British Railways green and crimson liveried carriage stock originating from the London Brighton & South Coast Railway and South Eastern & Chatham Railways. *A.E. Bennett*

With lifted safety valves indicating a full head of steam, 20 Shanklin barks away from Ryde St. John's Road under the signal gantry with a train for Ventnor on the 13th September 1964. The four semaphore signal arms on the gantry denote that St. John's Road signal box controls the two single line sections to Brading on the Ventnor line and Haven Street on the Cowes line. The signal box at Smallbrook Junction is closed and boarded up for the winter. *Roy Hobbs*

This is a view taken from the opposite side of the line from the shed yard on the 9th July 1960, looking towards Ryde Works on the right. 25 Godshill is about to depart with a train for Newport and Cowes, but note that Smallbrook Junction signal box must be open as this time the signal gantry has just two semaphore signal arms. Just out from the Works is a row of LBSCR open wagons that appear to have received new planks and are awaiting a coat of paint prior to return to service. *A.E. Bennett*

The Westinghouse pump on 24 Calbourne pants furiously whilst marshalling the carriage stock. On this occasion, Calbourne is driven by Ken West (who can be seen peering out from the cab) and fired by Ray Maxfield. It is the end of a long day for the crew and number 24 will soon be stabled on shed for the night with her simmering sisters. *Dr. J. Mackett*

Dr. John Mackett and Tim Genower were remarkable nocturnal Island railway photographers who captured magical moments of the steam railways in the hours of darkness.
Just soak up the atmosphere of this night shot of Ryde St John's Road in 1965. The warm glow from the signal box and illuminated station lamps reflecting on the shiny 60 foot rail lengths speak a thousand words. *Dr. J. Mackett*

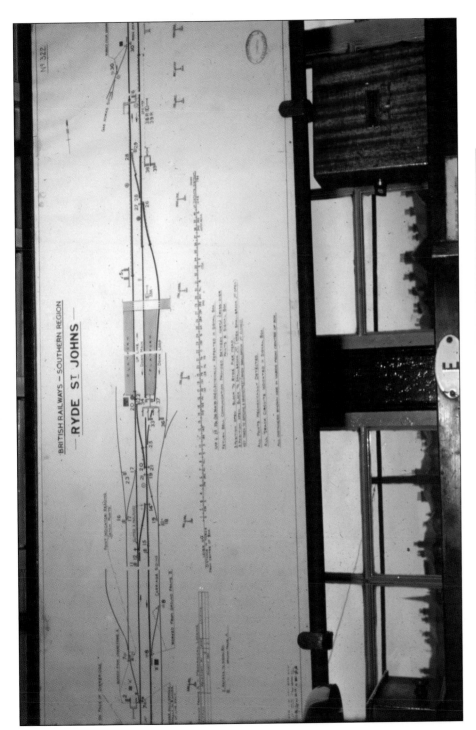

Ryde St. John's Road signal box lever frame and track signalling and point diagram on the 24th July 1962. This was the pride and glory of Signalmen: Dick Russell, Gordon Pointer and Reg Munday. These three signalmen were always very welcoming to young visitors like Andrew Britton with a drink and a biscuit. They would explain with great pride that 'their' wooden box originated from the South Eastern & Chatham Railway and was originally the Waterloo Junction signal box. It was re-erected on the Island by the Southern Railway in 1928 replacing the old North and South boxes. Before leaving the box to wander around the shed, one may even be allowed, unofficially and under strict guidance, to pull the levers for the next train, when Foreman Les Allen was out of sight!

Dr. J. Mackett

In the bottom left hand corner of this picture a busy gardener is seen digging his allotment next to Ryde St John's Road Shed. There was always a fine display of locomotives on parade awaiting entry to the Works or release into traffic. In this view taken in April 1961, from left to right on the 'No. 1 Loco Road', we can see E1 tank 4 Wroxall (withdrawn on the 22nd October 1960), 28 Ashey (entering the Works for Heavy Casual Overhaul on the 16th May 1961), Drummond boilered 27 Merstone (entering the Works on the 26th May 1961 for a General Overhaul and fitting of Adams boiler), 32 Bonchurch (ex Works on the 7th April 1961 following Light Intermediate Overhaul) and 35 Freshwater (stopped for brake assessment). *H. P. Mason*

A closer view of the sole remaining active Island E1 tank 4 Wroxall and O2 tank 32 Bonchurch at St John's Road Shed on 9th July 1960. The E1 tanks were powerful and sure footed engines that could handle most capably the coal traffic from Medina Wharf, general Island freight trains and, when called upon, occasional passenger trains. *A. E. Bennett*

'Blood sweat and filth' at the side of Ryde Shed as Coalman Jim Hewitt is pictured at the shovel. Fireman Tony Jones selects by hand some choice lumps of coal and Driver Bert Lock supervises from the footplate of Drummond boilered O2 tank 31 Chale. The coal capacity of an Island O2 tank was 3 tons and over 2 tons for an Island E1 tank. Following the closure of Newport Shed in 1957, Ryde St John's Shed had an allocation of twenty one engines, comprising of nineteen O2 tanks and two E1 tanks. To coal this mammoth locomotive stud there were the following coalmen: Jim Hewitt, Nobby Thomas, Frank Snow, George Prouten and Alf Mills, who worked a three shift pattern from 6am - 2pm, 2pm - 10pm and 10pm - 6am. When steam finished on 31st December 1966 this dirty and thankless job passed into history. *Tim R. Genower*

Fresh from the Works on the 10th September 1965, fully panelled seven compartment ex LBSCR brake second number S4157 from Set 488, just waiting for the electrical inspection of Ron Tewkesbury. Former Ryde Works carriage electrician Ron Tewkesbury outlined that from about 1948 the majority of the Island coaching stock consisted of ex LBSCR or SECR bogie vehicles. In latter years, following the closure of the Sandown - Newport line, these coaches were marshalled into eleven set trains, with the remaining vehicles standing spare. During the winter, all eleven sets were formed of three coach sets and were used indiscriminately on both the Cowes and Ventnor lines. For the summer timetable the seven Ryde based carriage sets: 490/1/2/3/4/7/500, were strengthened to six coach sets. The four Newport based sets: 485/6/7/8, were strengthened to four coach formations. All eleven coach sets were formed with one SEC brake second at the Ryde end of the train and one LBSC brake second at the Cowes/Ventnor end. The Ventnor sets were augmented in the summer was generally lighter and could carry more passengers than their SEC counterparts. The Brighton built stock with Brighton composites, while the Newport sets had heavier SEC composites. *Roy Hobbs*

Travelling inside the Island carriages was like stepping back in time - a unique experience. The SEC carriages were the most comfortable to ride in and this interior picture of a third class saloon taken in 1964 clearly shows the spacious bench layout, drop light door windows complete with leather straps, luggage racks and black & white pictures of Island scenes. *R.E. Burroughs*

18

According to former Ryde Works Chargehand Foreman Bill Smith and Boilersmith Joe Snellgrove, this hand operated Kirstall Forge built crane no 425S was one of the most useful pieces of equipment at Ryde Works. With its massive octagonal jib adorned at head and foot by some artistic castings, this crane had a 2 tons lifting capacity. It is pictured here next to the sheer legs lifting hoist on the 31st May 1962. Perhaps a lesser known unofficial use was to lift new young Works apprentices in indoctrination ceremonies! *Dr. J. Mackett*

Photographer Tim Genower has risen early from his former home at Wootton Rectory on a misty morning to capture this atmospheric shot of the double headed 7-50am parcels train to Shanklin. Accelerating away from Ryde St. John's Road are 20 Shanklin and 16 Ventnor with a passenger luggage van and converted SECR full brake van in tow. Two down trains from Ryde, the 7-40am Ryde Pier Head to Ventnor passenger train and the 7-50am parcels to Shanklin, were double-headed on Summer Saturdays. The second engine was attached at Ryde St John's Road in order to provide locomotives starting their day's work at Shanklin and Sandown. *Tim R. Genower*

Driver Jim Hunnybun has recorded on his working timetable and notes that he was at the regulator of 14 Fishbourne on this train the 5-07pm Ryde - Ventnor working. It is seen here heading away from Ryde towards Smallbrook Junction on the 4th September 1965. By this time 14 Fishbourne was the oldest active working steam locomotive in the country, being built in 1889. The majority Island O2 tanks had their own regular crews until February 1966. This fostered a greater degree of pride, care and maintenance and the regular allocated footplate men knew all their allocated engines' capabilities and faults. It is said that some Island engine drivers loved their engines as much as their wives! *A.E. Bennett*

Rostered Island locomotive working diagrams were allocated duty numbers and the engines were obliged to display duty numbers. The observation record and accompanying cine film from a second source reveal that this is the early morning 7:50am parcel train approaching Smallbrook. 24 Calbourne is on Duty 3 crewed by Driver Tony Tiltman and Fireman John Farrington and 29 Alverstone is on Duty 10 crewed by Driver Ted Dale and Fireman Andy Fryer with Guard Ron Childs at the rear on 10th July 1965. *A.E. Bennett*

By 6th August 1966 when this picture was taken preparations were being made for the sad demise of steam traction on the Isle of Wight. 22 Brading is approaching Smallbrook Junction with a Permanent Way train of bolster wagons, no doubt ready for conductor rail. This rail would be imported to the Isle of Wight via Medina Wharf and conveyed via the then closed Cowes line, ready for installation between Ryde and Shanklin. *Roy Hobbs*

Night time at Smallbrook Junction was always a special experience on warm balmy evenings, as one could hear nightjars and owls hooting in the neighbouring Whitefield Woods. On summer evenings it was possible to see glow worms alongside the track on the Cowes side of the box. The whole atmosphere of this isolated rural signal box took on a different character with primitive lighting and flickering paraffin illuminated signal lamps. For the regular signalmen: Vic Hailes, Eddie Spears and Ray Draper, the golden glow in the night sky from a steam locomotive cab and a cascade of red hot cinders from engine chimneys of passing trains continued to remind them that the railway activities did not cease in hours of darkness. It was truly a magical place of awe and wonder memories, so inspiring to the then young Andrew Britton.

Signalman Eddie Spears responds to the 'train in section' bells and readies himself to pull off the levers on the Smallbrook Junction knee frame levers in the midst of the night. He has no doubt exchanged a telephone conversation in his soft Northumbrian voice with neighbouring signalman Roy Way at Brading.

Driver Sonny 'Ginger' Minter on 20 Shanklin, passing at speed with a train from Ventnor, hands over the Brading - Smallbrook single line token to Signalman Eddie Spears. In the stillness of a summer night it was possible to hear a train climb up the 1 in 366 gradient from Brading and as the train approached through Whitefield Woods the engine exhaust would echo most eerily! After the train had passed the steam and smoke would linger along the line like the spectral shroud of a haunting ghost. *Tim R. Genever*

It is about mid-night at Smallbrook Junction on 16/17 September 1965. After the last train of the night had passed through, the annual procedure for closing Smallbrook Junction is underway. A Permanent Way trolley is loaded with the single line token instruments and the signal arms are removed ready for conveyance to Ryde St. John's Road. The whole operation is supervised by Mr W. A. 'Bill' Barton, the Island S & T Manager. Pictured from left to right are: Harold Sheaf (S & T Dept), Joe Primmer (Ryde Permanent Way Ganger), Steve Rustell S & T Spervisor), Cyril Henley (S & T Dept.), Fred 'The Squirrel' Chapman (S & T Dept.). *Dr. J. Mackett*

Soon Smallbrook Signal box is boarded up and locked for the winter with the points clipped and locked to allow the section to revert to two parallel single lines for operation. Harold Sheaf and Cyril Henley are pictured clipping the points. *Dr. J. Mackett*

Driver Eddie Prangnell leans out from the cab of 35 Freshwater to scoop up the token from the outstretched hand of Signalman Vic Hailes. According to Fireman Roger White who is at the regulator, Eddie would on occasions generously swap sides of the cab and have a go on the shovel to give his firemen experience of driving. After slowing to 10 mph for the token exchange the Cowes bound train will open up to build up speed to 45 mph as it heads away towards Ashey. *Dr. J. Mackett*

This is Driver Cyril Eason's view from the cab of 22 Brading as he slows down on the approach to Smallbrook Junction. Signalman Vic Hailes is ready and waiting to collect the single line token and has pulled off the inner home red signal for 22 Brading to pass. *Dr. J. Mackett*

Photographer Peter Mason had the great foresight to photograph each and every Island station, plus many bridges, level crossings, cuttings and viaducts in colour, including those closed prior to 1956. He also photographed Island steam trains in the landscape. This wonderful portrait taken near Ashey in August 1965 is perfectly framed by a hedge and tree. Peter was a most knowledgeable Island railway historian who was very keen to share his passion for the Island railways and encourage others. In so doing, Peter has ensured that this love of the Isle of Wight railways will continue for the future through his wonderful photography. *H. P. Mason*

Owing to subsidence of the original Ashey station platform and building, the track work was realigned along the course of the old loop line. 31 Chale waits patiently with a Cowes - Ryde train in the new brick built platform with its utilitarian shelter. The railway location is framed by a canopy of trees. Guard Tom Courtenay related from personal experience that the remote location of Ashey halt was a lonely place to be for a guard, especially when Driver 'Mad' Jack Sturgess was at the regulator of his regular engine 22 Brading. Driver Sturgess would try to get away fast on seeing the green flag and leave his guard stranded on the platform!" *R. E. Burroughs*

Fireman Ray Knapp peers out of 26 Whitwell waiting for the guard's green flag ready to depart from Haven Street with the Duty 13 11-25am Cowes - Ryde train on the 2nd July 1958. Signalman Jess Wheeler looks on. *H. P. Mason*

Fireman Stan 'Lester' Piggott on 25 Godshill on the 9-25am Ryde - Cowes trains exchanges the token with Haven Street Porter-Signalman Jess Wheeler on 1st August 1959. *H. P. Mason*

Relief Signalman Ron Coombes is pictured at the single line token instrument in Haven Street signal box on the 10th May 1959. *H. P. Mason*

It is October 1965 and Dr. John Mackett has arranged with the Haven Street signalmen Hughie White and Terry Wright to remove temporarily the signalling and point track diagram outside the front of the box in order to photograph it in daylight. *Dr. J. Mackett*

Taken from the top of the home signal on the 3rd July 1965, 20 Shanklin blows off steam from her safety valves at Haven Street ready for departure for Newport and Cowes. *G. S. Cocks*

In the garden at the opposite end of the station, Porter-Signalmen Hughie White and Terry Wright have been very busy ensuring the gardens look magnificent in July 1965. Photographer Tim Genower has photographed the highly prized Island 'Best Kept Station Competition' seat. The competition was introduced by the Southern Railway and continued by British Railways, being judged on station tidiness, and where possible, the station garden. The annual competition winners were presented with this special station seat recording the winning stations. Happily the seat is now preserved at Haven Street on the Isle of Wight Steam Railway. *Tim R. Genower*

Driver Ted Dale opens the regulator as 29 Alverstone storms up the gradient making an impressive start out of Haven Street. *David Peters*

Drummond boilered 22 Brading with a train bound for Haven Street and Ryde, heads through the cutting past the site of the original Wootton Station on the 30th August 1965. The right hand of Fireman Bob Church can be seen spraying the coal dust in the bunker, while Driver Denny Snow keeps a firm hand on the regulator. Meanwhile, Guard Jack Tharme can be pictured looking through the left hand window of the SEC brake second coach behind engine 22. *Barry J. Eagles*

33

Peering through the left hand side cab spectacle of 33 Bembridge can be seen Driver Harry 'Toby' Watson with a Cowes bound train descending down the 1 in 64 gradient past the site of the former station at Whippingham on the 3rd July 1965. *G. S. Cocks*

No. 28 Ashey drifts down the gradient just before entering the 73 yard long Newport Tunnel with a train for Cowes. *Dr. J. Mackett*

No. 21 Sandown was the pride and joy of drivers Gerald Coombes and Eddie Prangnell. We are unable to determine which driver is at the controls on this occasion, despite digital computer enhancement of the cab spectacle. Both drivers were outstanding enginemen and loved their faithful steed. Eddie was known to even paint the interior of Sandown's cab. Hundreds of train spotters knew this driver as 'Uncle Eddie' for he would often give unofficial footplate rides on 21 Sandown in return for a donation to the Southern Railway Children Homes. Over the years Eddie Prangnell raised hundreds of pounds for this charity. Sandown is seen bursting out of Newport Tunnel on Duty 4 with a train for Cowes. *David Peters*

The Newport - Sandown line having being closed, one of the two drawbridges over the River Medina was removed in 1963. The picture shows it is high tide and that the drawbridge had been opened by hand, the section of track sliding on rollers to allow the XXXX barge to pass upstream to the local brewery. Two railway staff peer down from the drawbridge eagerly awaiting the passing of the barge, although shipping had priority over trains. *Dr. J. Mackett*

After the barge had passed, the final operation was to replace the fishplates and reconnect the signal wires. Permanent Way Ganger Arthur 'Arty' Strickland is seen tightening the fish plate bolts after the drawbridge has been closed. *Dr. J. Mackett*

With the XXXX barge safely moored up on the other side of the drawbridge, 26 Whitwell heads out of Newport bunker first to Ryde. *Dr. J. Mackett*

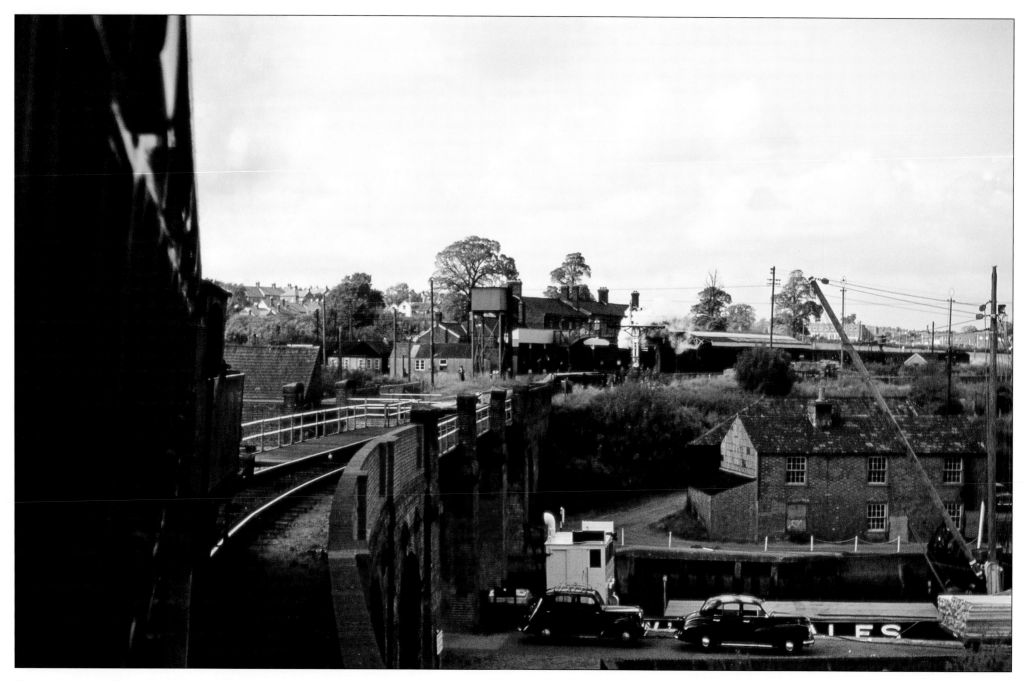

We are on board a Ryde - Cowes train entering Newport across the sharply curved viaduct before crossing over the River Medina drawbridge on the 1st October 1965. Waiting for our arrival is a Ryde bound train. Down below us on the right are two vintage vehicles parked alongside a barge. On the left is a Vauxhall 14 and on the right is a Morris Six Wolsey which was sold for £672 when new. *David Janes*

Suitably replenished with water for its tanks, 30 Shorwell waits under the footbridge for a clear road to depart for Haven Street with the daily freight. On the extreme right of this picture are the carriage service men Messrs. Holbrook, Tilley and Chiverton busy at work in the carriage sidings. *Dr. J. Mackett*

Taken from the footbridge we are able to view 17 Seaview with an approaching with a train from Cowes, as passengers wait patiently under the awning of the up platform at Newport, on the 4th August 1965. Fireman John Howe peers out of the cab whilst his regular driver on 17 Seaview, Doug Saunders, applies the Westinghouse brakes. The building on the left was at this time still the headquarters to Mr Gardiner, Assistant for the Isle of Wight Railways and the administration staff. *R.E. Burroughs/ Colin Elvers Collection*

A view looking up Newport station from the Cowes end finds E1 tank 4 Wroxall engaged in shunting activities on the 9th July 1960. She had no doubt been hauling a coal train to and from Medina Wharf on Duty 11 during the morning. *A.E. Bennett*

The impressive exterior of Newport Station on the 13th July 1963, showing, parked on the left, an Austin Cambridge XDL 165 which was registered on the Island in August/September 1961. On the right we see a Standard Vanguard estate model, manufactured in 1950/51. *H. P. Mason*

This conversation piece at Newport Station on the 29th October 1965, shows Driver Doug Saunders in the cab of 24 Calbourne pictured talking to Permanent Way Ganger Tom Becky, while Fireman John Howe listens attentively. Could they be discussing if they have encountered the escaped horses en route from Ashey, an event which is recorded in the train register for that day? *Roy Hobbs*

A truly atmospheric photograph showing the Cowes train departing from Newport Station. The Station Foreman Arthur Day is pictured bending over reading the labels on the parcels left on the platform. An unidentified colleague looks on with plenty of back-breaking work ahead. *R. E. Burroughs*

A sad view showing the demolition of Newport Shed in progress on the left of the photograph as Fireman Bob Church peers out from the cab of 20 Shanklin as it departs for Cowes on 16th June 1962. *A. E. Bennett*

No. 27 arrives at Newport with one of the two daily coal trains from Medina Wharf on the Friday 10th September 1965. After running around the wagons, the locomotive will shunt across the main lines where it will propel the wagons into the sidings and Freshwater yard for unloading by local coal merchants. *Roy Hobbs*

An action shot taken from the steps of Newport North signal box shows Signalman Ron 'Snozzle' Bennett collecting the single line token from Fireman Ron Brett as he passes by on a train from Cowes. Driver Sonny 'Ginger' Minter is pictured on the other side of the footplate of 26 Whitwell. Ron was a very jolly and warm hearted signalman who was most welcoming. Occasionally when in a hurry, he had been known to exchange the token with passing train crews by leaning out of the signal box window with the token attached to the end of a broom stick! *Dr. J. Mackett*

This time Dr. John Mackett is at line side with his camera to capture Signalman Jim Hooper exchanging the token with Fireman Ken Simmonds on 28 Ashey heading away towards Cowes. *Dr. J. Mackett*

A four coach Cowes bound train headed by 14 Fishbourne emerges out from the reeds crossing over Cement Mills viaduct in 1965. With the closure of the mills in 1944, the pond was steadily reclaimed by nature through vegetation and sediment. *Tim R Genower*

No. 29 Alverstone shuts off steam for the 10 mph speed restriction, resulting in the safety valves lifting. The O2 tank is pictured heading for Cowes with a four coach set and a 'swinger'. The Cement Mills viaduct had nine spans with wrought iron plate girders, longitudinal timbers, timber decking with cast iron columns and brick abutments. Although it was strengthened with extra piling in June 1926, the structure was never considered satisfactory for full line speed and the 10 mph speed restriction was enforced until the line closed in February 1966. *David Peters*

With a strong cross wind to battle against, an unidentified O2 tank heads her typical four coach set for Mill Hill and Cowes along the banks of the River Medina near Werrar, in March 1965. The lonely telegraph poles perched on the embankment with the traditional lineside fencing were so characteristic of the railway scene - so dramatically captured in this timeless picture. *Tim R. Genower*

Cement Mills Halt was just over a mile north of Newport. It was used mainly by fishermen and workers at the local Medina commercial undertakings. Intending passengers could hail a train to halt by a simple wave. Passengers who wished to alight from a train were required to advise the guard at the previous stop. The concrete shelter and 65 foot timber platform were less than inviting and the siding was long abandoned when this view was taken, although its final use was as a location for the scrapping of O2 tank 18 Ningwood in 1966. *R.E. Burroughs*

The Medina estuary was a superb photographic location for railway photographers. Tim Genower's outstanding picture has it all as we glance across the fields to witness a passing three coach Cowes bound train. In the background almost totally masked by the steam from the chimney is the Paddle Steamer Medway Queen, moored in East Medina Mill Pond, having arrived there on the 28th September, 1965. *Tim R. Genower*

At approximately the same location near Werrar Farm Occupation Crossing alongside the Medina estuary we see a Medina Wharf - Newport coal train, made up of LBSCR open wagons complete with two ex LSWR brake vans. We are able to view the whole train - an everyday sight at the time. *Tim R. Genower*

For O2 tanks with a heavy coal train, the struggle up the 1 in 60 gradient from Medina Wharf quay up to the main line presented a real challenge for the crews, particularly in unfavourable weather conditions. All drivers would make sure the locomotive sand boxes were full prior to leaving the shed ready for extra adhesion under the wheels. *Dr. J. Mackett*

In latter years the tracks were neglected and weeds began to grow and take over. Crews had to take extra care therefore when shunting. Here we see a Cowes bound train passing the Wharf on the main line. *Dr. J. Mackett*

A simple fifteen foot wooden platform with an electric light was provided for the workers at Medina Wharf Halt. Trains only stopped at this halt if prior request was made to the guard, and it was necessary to occupy the carriage compartment next to the locomotive. To make the return trip, it was possible to stop the train by flagging down the driver as we see in this picture of a Ryde bound train slowing to collect a lone passenger. *H. P. Mason*

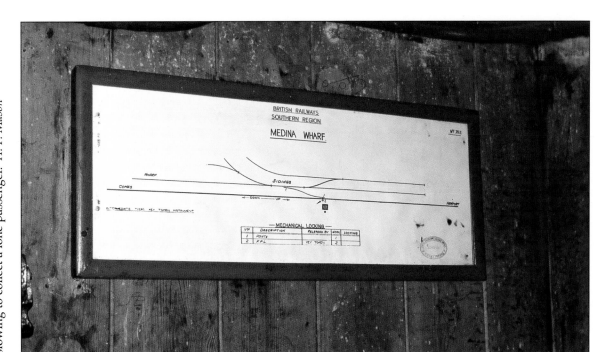

The junction leading to the Wharf was controlled by a ground frame adjacent to the main line. An intermediate instrument token allowed trains from the Wharf to enter the Cowes - Newport line, following clearance from Newport North signal box. *Tim R. Genower*

A general view of Medina Wharf sidings, complete with the Duty 11 O2 tank 30 Shorwell, which is busy at work shunting on the 15th August 1959. This O2 tank emerged from Ryde Works on the 17th July 1959 after a Light Overhaul. She was still 'running in' when required to substitute for E1 tank 4 Wroxall, which was on Ryde shed for a routine boiler wash out. When the Southern Railway took over in 1923 there were over 500 wagons on the Isle of Wight. Many of them could be found at work in the Wharf at any one time in various states of repair. Note also the two barges on the right of the picture. *H. P. Mason*

Smithards Lane level crossing was the last public-gated crossing on the Isle of Wight railways. The last full time crossing keeper when the line was open was Mrs. M. S. Bennett, who lived in the crossing cottage. She always kept the main gates closed against the road. Mrs. Bennett would explain to objecting motorists that the reason for this was that the railway had only been required to provide an occupational crossing on farmland when the line was originally opened. Locals usually found it more expedient to drive round past Mill Hill station. *Tim R. Genower*

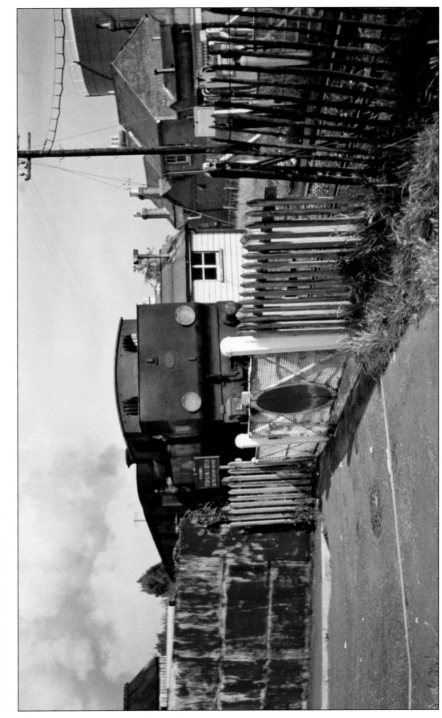

No. 33 Bembridge is approaching bunker first, having just left Mill Hill station with a train for Newport and Ryde. Mrs. Bennett would emerge from her cottage on the ring of the automatic bell to pull the lever locking the pedestrian gates. Smithards Lane Crossing was protected by red armed home signals only. Even after the passenger train service ceased, Smithards Lane Crossing was manned during daylight hours for some months by Porter-Signalman Hughie White to cover freight service traffic to and from Cowes, following Mrs Bennett's retirement. *R. E. Burroughs*

55

With three waiting passengers on the curved platform at Mill Hill for the approaching train from Cowes, we look northwards towards the gloomy 208 yard tunnel. We can see the 1880 station building, complete with the original 1871 wooden building. To anyone wishing to construct a model of an Isle of Wight railway scene, Mill Hill with its sharply curved platform and tunnel provides a simple but achievable possibility. *R. E. Burroughs*

Even though Mill Hill was less than half a mile from the terminus at Cowes, it was a busy commuter station at certain times of the day. Here we see the Cowes bound 28 Ashey. The platform duties were shared by Leading Porters Arthur Darke and Horace Cade, who appeared to know all the regular passengers at their station. These two gentlemen would even hold a train in the platform to wait for one of their late regulars! Where else but on the Isle of Wight would this practice go on? *R. E. Burroughs*

This photograph portrays something of the character of the Isle of Wight railways in a typical Island town setting as we see Fireman Jim Arnott on 27 Merstone coasting down the 1 in 67 gradient into Cowes across St. Mary's Road bridge. "Too low for buses" proclaims the painted sign on the trough girder bridge. On the right of the picture we see a Nash Metropolitan 1400cc car with an A50 engine, which was available in Britain with right hand drive from October 1956. A pushbike leans against the curb on the left hand side. *Tim R. Genower*

With the benefit of computer digital enhancement it has been possible to identify clearly the smiling face of Driver Eddie Prangnell looking out through the driver's cab spectacle of his regular engine 21 Sandown on Duty 6. This view was taken from Granville Bridge looking along the cutting towards St Mary's Road underbridge, in October 1962. *Dr. J. Mackett*

Looking down the gradient into Cowes station from the signal box in October 1962, the two coal wharves on the left look very busy with fresh deliveries in the LBSCR open wagons ready for unloading from Medina Wharf. *Dr. J. Mackett*

Having run around the train, 32 Bonchurch prepares to depart for Newport and Ryde. The fireman is building up the fire and the safety valves are just lifting ready for the stiff climb out of Cowes. *Dr. J. Mackett*

In 'Ryde by Steam Volume One' on page 80, Roy Hobbs captured the S.S. United States passing 24 Calbourne at Cowes with the caption, "The Lady and the Liner". This was thought to be the only picture of its kind. David Peters saw this remarkable picture and delved through his superb archive of colour slides to rediscover this remarkable view. Next stop Le Havre, for the 1,035 feet, 66,348 ton liner S.S. France, which is seen passing Cowes station. On closer inspection the cameraman appears to have photographed another interesting occurrence as 26 Whitwell is running around its carriages in Platform 2 instead of the usual Platform 1. *David Peters*

A delightfully clean 29 Alverstone runs around her train on Duty 8 from Platform 1 at Cowes on 5th June 1965. The train operation at Cowes was particularly interesting for the railway enthusiast to watch. Firstly after arrival and uncoupling, the locomotive would back the train up the platform. Next the engine would run forward and then reverse over the crossover to the adjacent line and out to the station approaches. The guard in the brake coach would then release the hand-brake which allowed the coaches to roll gently down the gradient towards the buffers. The engine followed behind. This was an everyday working practice, but totally illegal! On Cowes Fireworks Night was on, three complete trains would wait ready to leave as soon as the passengers returned to the station following the conclusion of the display. *David Janes*

After walking from the Red Funnel steamer at West Cowes Fountain Pier and up to Terminus Road, passengers had to climb the entrance steps, before entering the spacious concourse of Cowes Station. Photographer and author Barry Eagles has captured the scene to perfection on the 27th October 1965. From left to right, we can view the entrance at the top of the steps, the parcels and cloakroom, the chalked time table departures next to the ticket booking office, the station clock, the general and ladies' room, and, to complete the scene, the distinctive wooden flower tubs with the white signwritten name proudly proclaiming, "Cowes". In the summer season, hanging baskets of flowers hung from the rafters of the generously glazed roof, making this a memorable place to commence or conclude a journey on the Isle of Wight railways. *Barry J. Eagles*

This is the exterior of Cowes station on the 3rd November 1961, taken from Carvel Lane. The station terminus was situated on the side of a hill making it rather inconvenient for ferry passengers, particularly if they had luggage to drag up on a hot summer day or in pouring rain. A gate for parcel traffic was provided at platform level on Terminus Road and was used daily for newspaper and postal traffic. A car spotter taking numbers has a feast of vintage vehicle registration numbers to record. They are from left to right: a Thames Trader lorry, a white Hillman Minx Tourer, red Ford Model Y Woody BDL 289 (Island registered in 1937), a white Austin van and a Standard Vanguard GDL 238 (Island registered in 1949). *H. P. Mason*

We return to Smallbrook Junction to view, from the top of the inner home signal on the Cowes line, 27 Merstone bound for the next stop at Brading. *Tim R. Genower*

The sweet scent of coconut perfume is in the air from the yellow gorse at Truckells Bridge on the route south of Smallbrook Junction. Here Drummond boilered 22 Brading is climbing at 1 in 134 through the delightful countryside of Whitefield Woods. *Tim R. Genower*

28 Ashey approaches Truckells Bridge at speed, with possibly Driver Peter Mills at the controls, on the longest single line section on the Ventnor line. Popularly known to enginemen as 'Pheasant Alley', it no doubt provided many a tasty meal when the unfortunate game bird decided to walk in front of a passing train. In the autumn it was possible to see red squirrels gathering nuts in the trees. *Dr. J. Mackett*

No. 17 Seaview is pictured at the head of an unusual mixed parcel-freight train heading for Ryde. The parcels section is made up of a converted SECR full brake, a PMV van and a second SECR full brake. Attached at the rear are three open LBSCR coal wagons and double balcony brake van S56058 of LSWR origin. *Tim R. Genower*

31 Chale with the 12:10 Ryde Pier Head - Ventnor train drifts down the bank through the cutting near Wall Lane bridge with the regulator shut on Sunday 13th June 1964. A picture taken by a different photographer at Ventnor of this same train reveals that 31 Chale is being driven by Maurice Prouten and fired by Terry Humber, with Larry 'Lofty' Eklund as guard of the six coach set.
Tim Stephens

Signalman Roy Way waits to collect the Smallbrook-Brading token from Fireman Joe Moore on 31 Chale, which is seen hauling the 10-10am Ryde-Ventnor train on the 25th May, 1963. Driver Maurice Prouten, who is driving 31 Chale, and his colleagues were highly skilled experts in the art of a fast approach using the Westinghouse air brakes, followed by a safe and precise stop at the platform - even on a falling gradient like this one at Brading. *H. P. Mason*

Drummond boilered 22 Brading driven by Denny Snow arrives at Brading with the 4-20pm train to Shanklin on the 25th May 1963. On the left, just off the picture, is the Station Master's House lived in by Isle of Wight Area Inspector Ron Russell. Ron is knowledgeable about every aspect of the Island railways and has the reputation of always being so welcoming with cool ginger beer on scorching hot summer days. On the extreme right of this panoramic view we can see the signal box. Note the gas lights which added a touch of romance to the scene. *H. P. Mason*

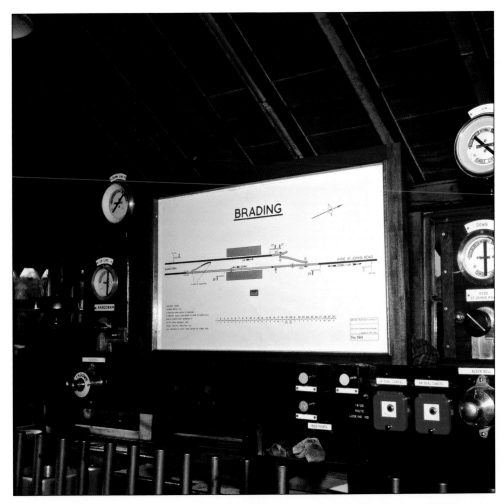

Inside Brading signal box we can see the lever frame and the signal and point diagram. This was the pride and joy of the resident signalmen Roy Way and Jess Wheeler in steam days. The box was isolated and when this photograph was taken most of the 30 levers were disused. Although the Bembridge Branch closed on 21st September 1953, the line to St. Helen's Quay was retained until the 17th November, 1957. During this period the line was used to transfer withdrawn carriage stock and wagons for dismantling at the quay. *Dr. J. Mackett*

This is an idyllic scene near Yarbridge on the Sandown side of Brading. Here we see children fishing oblivious to a Ventnor bound train rushing past on the double track on the 22nd August 1964.
H. P. Mason

A rare view of the south bound Ventnor freight headed by 35 Freshwater at Yarbridge. *David Peters*

Approaching Sandown on the double track from Brading is 16 Ventnor on Duty 11 while passing bunker first is Ryde bound 35 Freshwater on Duty 10 on the 3rd July 1965. *A. E. Bennett*

This picture is taken from above eye level as we see 31 Chale leaving Sandown with a five coach train containing a mixture of green and crimson liveried carriage stock, on the 16th April 1960. On the right we see Sandown freight sidings and the remains of the former line to Merstone and Newport. Behind the Ryde bound train we can view Sandown station with the signal box perched above the canopy on the up platform. *A. E. Bennett*

The firebox door is doubtless rattling on No. 28 Ashey as she makes a brisk start and accelerates away with a heavy train from Sandown for Ryde on the 18th July 1964. *A. E. Bennett*

No. 32 Bonchurch begins the demanding 1 in 80 climb which commences from the south end of Sandown station towards Los Altos Park, Lake and Shanklin on the 14th July 1960. On the left hand side of this picture is the former bay platform, once used for trains to Merstone and Newport. The foot crossing in the foreground was a particularly dangerous place. Author Andrew Britton vividly recalls a very near miss when approaching the station on the footplate of 24 Calbourne in the company of Driver Ken West and Fireman Ray Maxfield, when a pedestrian deliberately ignored repeated blasts of 24's hooter and decided to dash across in front of them! *A. E. Bennett*

Looking down the lane towards the foot crossing just outside Sandown station, we see 14 Fishbourne masked by the traditional Southern wooden station fencing on the 3rd September 1960. This was a familiar scene never to be forgotten. *A. E. Bennett*

Los Altos Park was a very popular place for enthusiasts to photograph and sound record the engines working flat out. Here we see 32 Bonchurch giving her all with plenty of smoke and an almost deafening exhaust. The driver is 'Mad' Jack Sturgess (not on his regular 22 Brading) and Fireman Tony Toogood. True to form Driver Sturgess spotted the helpless photographer Peter Mason, whom he knew very well, and sprayed him with the engine peep pipe! *H. P. Mason*

Returning tourists often queued four deep in the streets in the 1950s and 60s for trains outside Shanklin station, as shown on this busy scene on the 12th August 1961. Holidays makers alight from a Seaview Services coach, while a fleet of classic car taxis have plenty of trade. From left to right they are: an Austin Taxi FX4, an Armstrong Sidley Whitley (dating from 1949) and an Austin 18 Taxi GMK 930 (originally registered in Middlesex in September/October 1938). *H. P. Mason*

This is the view from the rear side window of the Shanklin signal box with a train entering from Sandown, which Signalman Ted Johnson is waiting to greet for token exchange on the platform on the 13th June 1959. *H. P. Mason*

In December 1966, on the down platform at Shanklin, we see the unusual spectacle of 22 Brading taking water from the station fire hydrant having run around the carriage stock. *D. J. Mitchell*

No. 24 Calbourne has just arrived at Shanklin with a train from Ryde. The fireman will now be hard at the shovel to build up a good head of steam ready for the assault on Apse Bank. Immediately on leaving Shanklin platform the 1 in 70 climb for one and a half miles commenced. *R. E. Burroughs*

With a plume of dark smoke, No. 21 Sandown with Driver Gerald Coombes at the regulator, is now well into her all out attack of Apse Bank, having just passed under Cliff Bridge. *David Peters*

No. 24 Calbourne gets to grips with Apse Bank as it storms through Hyde Cutting and makes a glorious sight with the 6:05pm Ryde-Ventnor train on the 15th June 1961. No doubt the thunderous regular rhythm of the exhaust note is echoing through the surrounding woodland. *H. P. Mason*

The view from Three Arch Bridge near Wroxall on the 28th August 1965 as a train from Ventnor rounds the long forty seven chain curve from Winstone, around St Martin's Down. Behind the train is the glorious, picturesque down land which was such a feature from the carriage window. *A. E. Bennett*

Fireman Terry Hatcher can be seen on the fireman's side of the cab taking a well earned rest on his regular engine, 18 Ningwood, almost at the top of Apse Bank on the 1 in 108 gradient just before Wroxall. His regular mate, Driver Frank Ash, is at the regulator on the 13th September 1964. *Roy Hobbs*

This superb panoramic photograph was taken from Cook's Castle in July 1962, and shows an O2 tank hauling an 'up' Ventnor-Ryde Pier Head train away from Wroxall, down the gradient. *H. P. Mason*

How do you exchange tokens when you already have a train in the platform? Wroxall signalman Dick Randall shows how as 24 Calbourne passes through with a train for Ventnor.
R. E. Burroughs/Colin Elvers Collection

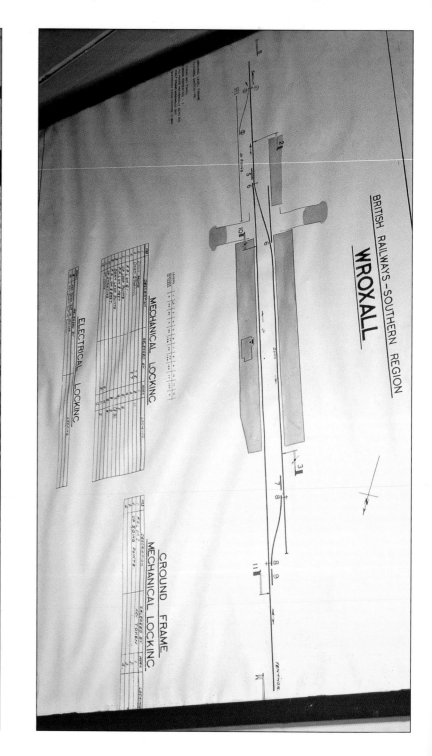

Inside Wroxall signal box on the up platform, showing the lever frame and signalling & point diagram. The resident signalmen, Dick Randall and Harold Unstead, were proud of their signal box and were always polishing and cleaning to perfection. On a rare occasion Harold Unstead overslept one morning thus delaying the morning train. He blamed his cheese and onion sandwiches for giving him a bad night's sleep! However, as Andrew Britton can testify, Harold was a kind and generous man who was always willing to share the contents of his lunch box with visiting young railway enthusiasts who had left their own provisions on the train! *Dr. J. Mackett*

St. Boniface Down provides the backcloth as Ventnor bound 33 Bembridge awaits the arrival of an incoming train. *R. E. Burroughs/ Colin Elvers Collection*

With Driver Alf Goodson at the controls, 22 Brading makes a spirited getaway to Ventnor from the 370 feet down platform at Wroxall on the 13th September 1964. *Roy Hobbs*

Framed by the arch of Wroxall Manor Road Bridge, which is eleven miles and forty nine chains from Ryde Pier Head, 31 Chale bursts out of the tunnel into daylight, engulfing the cutting with steam. *David Peters*

We are on the footplate of 22 Brading looking out from Driver Cyril Eason's view ahead towards the north portal of Ventnor Tunnel. Climbing the final 1 in 88 we will soon plunge into the smoky depths of the 1312 yard Ventnor Tunnel. Once inside the dark, sooty, damp tunnel, approximately one third of the way into the tunnel, Driver Eason will look out for the shaft of light from the tunnel vent set high above on St. Boniface Down, which will shine down on 22 Brading's Drummond dome. During the hours of darkness drivers had to count as they passed over the 26 joints of rail and feel the fresh cold air from the tunnel vent. From the tunnel vent, drivers of steam trains had to count a further 36 rail joints before the exit of the tunnel into Ventnor station. On passing the 30th rail joint, the train should have been approaching the home signal. This was the cue for the fireman of 22 Brading to prepare to exchange the single line token with the Ventnor signalman from the left hand side of the engine immediately upon exiting the tunnel mouth. *Dr. J. Mackett*

Taken from above the station on St. Boniface Down, we see the classic view of 30 Shorwell leaving Ventnor for Ryde on the 30th August, 1965. The station site was cut out of the chalk, but even then this terminus was 294 feet above sea level. *A. E. Bennett*

This picture is taken from ground level next to Ventnor signal box and shows No. 30 Shorwell, with the Westinghouse air brakes being applied, about to burst out into daylight from Ventnor Tunnel with an inbound train from Ryde. Having run round its train in Ventnor station, the locomotive had to retreat into the tunnel in order to regain access to the platform. In the smoke-filled darkness, the problem for the loco crew was not knowing when the signalman had reset the points. When shunting wagons, some loco crews shunted right back into the tunnel and it was impossible to listen out for a bell before setting back or look out for a green flag. Inspector Ron Russell therefore had installed a set of colour light markers at intervals and a colour light signal. *Dr. J. Mackett*

This picture taken from outside the goods shed at the north end of Ventnor station on the 5th September 1965 shows the chalk cliffs surrounding the tunnel entrance in all their glory. Signalman Sid Sartin has just collected the token from Fireman Charlie Hackett on 35 Freshwater. Meanwhile, a porter prepares to collect the incoming parcels from the end brake coach. Soaring overhead and in the many craggy rocks are the resident rooks, squabbling and cawing raucously. For cliff-loving birds, Ventnor station was a sheltered paradise and added to the special sounds of this spacious theatre of steam. *D. J. Mitchell*

From under the station canopy we see a Morris 1000 Royal Mail van actually on Ventnor platform loading the post. Meanwhile Driver Roy Dyer on 27 Merstone waits patiently ready for the postman to complete his duties. *D. J. Mitchell*

The portable gangway was still the only means of access for passengers to the island platform at Ventnor until the station closed on the 17th April 1966. Special safety instructions were set out for use of this portable bridge whereby a bell code was exchanged with the signalman to indicate that the line was obstructed. No. 33 Bembridge is pictured on the left of the picture, resting in the shadow of the island platform canopy. *Dr. J. Mackett*

The Isle of Wight railway system came up for closure on Sunday 3rd October 1965 and photographer David Janes decided to take one last journey to the Island on Friday 1st October. At Ventnor, 20 Shanklin enters the sidings with a short freight to shunt and collect stored railway carriages and any railway items for return to Ryde. The LCGB ran a special planned last train on the Sunday, but in the event the closure of the Shanklin-Ventnor section was postponed. *David Janes*

The Isle of Wight became a very popular place to visit for railway enthusiasts in the final years of steam traction. The Locomotive Club of Great Britain ran the first of three special trains on the 4th October 1964, "The Vectis Rail Tour". Here we see Fireman Terry Hatcher taking water on 14 Fishbourne, while Driver Tony Tiltman is seen operating the control wheel of the water column at ground level. Guard Sam Wells is directing the crowd of photographers in the yard near the tunnel mouth. On returning to Ryde the train was hauled by 28 Ashey for the second leg of the tour to Newport and Cowes. Unfortunately, owing to 22 Brading dropping a side rod near Smithard's Lane, the tour had to terminate prematurely at Newport. *Peter Paye*

This is a superb view looking down through the trees from the path at the south end of Ventnor station on the 5th September 1965. Fireman Charlie Hackett cleans out the ash filled smokebox of 35 Freshwater, while Driver John Townson attends to replenishing engine water tanks. *D. J. Mitchell*

After much detective work and consultation with the residents of Ventnor, Colin Elvers and vintage vehicle expert David Unitt have discovered a tremendous amount of detail about this nostalgic picture. Taken at the entrance to Ventnor station on the 5th September 1965, it reveals a hive of activity with a collection of vintage vehicles. Fireman Charlie Hackett is busy continuing to clean out the smokebox ashes from 35 Freshwater, while Driver John Townson attends to the engine requirements. From left to right we see Ventnor based taxis: grey two tone Austin Cambridge XDL 524 owned by the Royal Garage (registered on the Island in 1962), black Austin 16 CUL 41 owned by Leslie's Taxis (registered in London in 1936), maroon Zodiac owned by Leslie's Taxis, black Zephyr (partially obscured behind the Consul) owned by Leslie's Taxis, black Zephyr RFY 438 owned by Nash's Garage, two tone white Austin Cambridge YDL 568 owned by Royal Garage with its driver Frank Dixon opening the taxi door(registered on the Island in 1962), two tone Consul on the far right is 3289 PO owned by Leslie's Taxis (registered in West Sussex in 1959), two tone consul owned by Leslie's garage and centre in the foreground is black Consul SCG 182 owned by Randall's Taxis (registered in Glasgow in 1957). Railwayman Porter Signalman Alec Widger is pictured near the station entrance holding on to a canopy beam. He was also the last booking clerk at Ventnor West station in 1952.

By a sad coincidence Driver John Townson was the person to drive the final train from Ventnor on the 17th April, 1966 and so, for the last time, returned to Ryde by steam.

D. J. Mitchell/ COLOUR RAIL